I AM

Worthy

UNCOVERING OUR FAULTY
CORE BELIEFS TO FIND
HEALTH & RESILIENCE
ROOTED IN TRUTH

MACEE WHATLEY, LMHC

WESTBOW
PRESS®
A DIVISION OF THOMAS NELSON
& ZONDERVAN

WestBow Press books may be ordered through booksellers or by contacting:

WestBow Press
A Division of Thomas Nelson & Zondervan
1663 Liberty Drive
Bloomington, IN 47403
www.westbowpress.com
844-714-3454

ISBN: 978-1-6642-8017-5 (sc)
ISBN: 978-1-6642-8018-2 (hc)
ISBN: 978-1-6642-8016-8 (e)

Library of Congress Control Number: 2022918569

Print information available on the last page.

WestBow Press rev. date: 10/24/2022

NEW SEASON. FRESH PERSPECTIVE.

Since 2008, my work with clients has led me to look at how our core beliefs affect our self-worth. I have seen how deep-seated beliefs run the show in the background without many of us realizing why we respond to various situations in the ways we do. Not only have I seen this concept in my daily work, it is something I have personally worked through heavily in the course of my lifetime. I have learned that I am continually drawn back to who God created me to be, and I remind myself of the truth He has spoken into my life. The more able we are to recognize our worth in the eyes of the Creator, the more our responses will line up with the truth we are rooted in.

My desire is for everyone to know and appreciate their worth. My faith in God has been a journey, and I continue to grow deeper in my relationship with Him. When we take time to focus on digging deeper into our stories and how God can use us, we allow healing, growth, and change to take place.

The goal of this journal is to give you the skills and tools to be introspective and self-directive in your journey toward self-worth that is grounded in your relationship with God. My prayer is for you to be secure in who you are in every aspect. If you are having difficulty finding direction or need some guidance, my hope is that God's words will speak to you and direct you in this process.

EACH PAGE OF THIS WORKBOOK WILL CONSIST OF:

- an *I am worthy of* statement. Take time to sit with this statement, and gauge its truth in whatever season you're in.
- a journal prompt. Find a quiet place and reflect on the prompt. I want you to be honest with yourself. Powerful things are birthed out of honesty. Make a change. Do something different—something new.
- a Scripture reference. Our goal is to become rooted in truth and we need scripture to back that up.

  There are three steps to applying scripture to our lives:
  Read. Write. Pray.
  —Read it.
  —Write out what it means to you.
  —Pray it over your life.

I hope these statements and prompts guide you on your journey to healthy self-worth grounded in God's absolute truth.

...of grace.

JOURNAL PROMPT

Do you give yourself grace when you fall, fail, or miss expectations you've set for yourself? How healthy are your expectations?

It's time to reframe expectations. List the expectations you hold of yourself as well as the ones you feel others have of you. Reflect on what needs you're trying to fill. When we're disappointed in things, it's generally because we're not filling our needs in a healthy way. It's time to learn that failure is not fatal. Allow yourself to try without the fear of failure.

SCRIPTURE
Ephesians 2:4–9

Journal

...of investing in myself.

JOURNAL PROMPT

Do you find that you put yourself on the back burner? Do you tell yourself that there's time to work on and invest in yourself after everyone else is taken care of? We begin to uncover our worth when we understand that God wants us to do things that fill us up instead of constantly feeling drained by always doing for others. What is one thing you can do right now that your future self will thank you for? It could be a financial, emotional, mental, or relational change.

Think of ways to invest in yourself now instead of waiting for the right time. Begin implementing your action steps today. Don't let the allure of waiting for a new day rob you of something good now.

SCRIPTURE
Proverbs 24:27

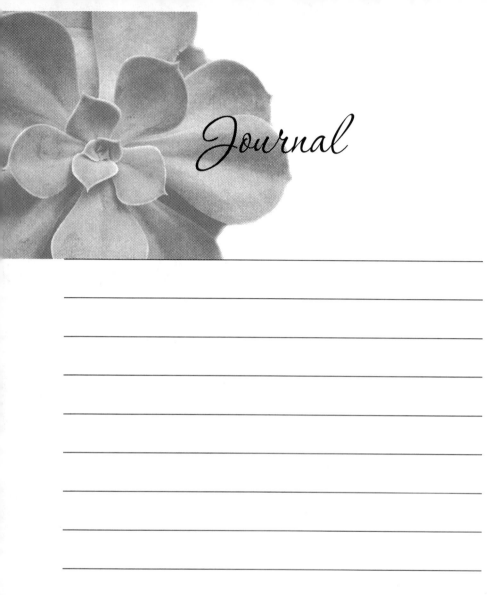

Journal

...of understanding myself.

JOURNAL PROMPT

Finish the phrase "I Am ..." What comes to mind? Do you believe you are worthy, lovable, valuable? Where is the evidence?

Starting to understand your core beliefs is your first step to truly understanding who you are. When we have faulty core beliefs—damaging things that people have spoken into our lives / lies we've bought into— our behavior cycles will continue to find ways to fulfill these beliefs. We begin to discover our core beliefs by asking ourselves what our actions say about us and if we truly believe those beliefs are still beneficial to us now.

SCRIPTURE
Romans 12:2

Journal

...of being loved.

JOURNAL PROMPT

List and discuss three reasons you deserve to be loved. Is that too difficult? If so, write down three things that someone has said or done that made you feel you didn't deserve to be loved. Why does this person get to speak into the core of who you are?

Everyone deserves to feel worthy of being loved. When it comes down to it, you were so broken that Somebody had to die for you, but you are so loved that Somebody did! Allow Jesus to speak into Your life and reveal just how loved you are.

SCRIPTURE
Romans 5:6–11

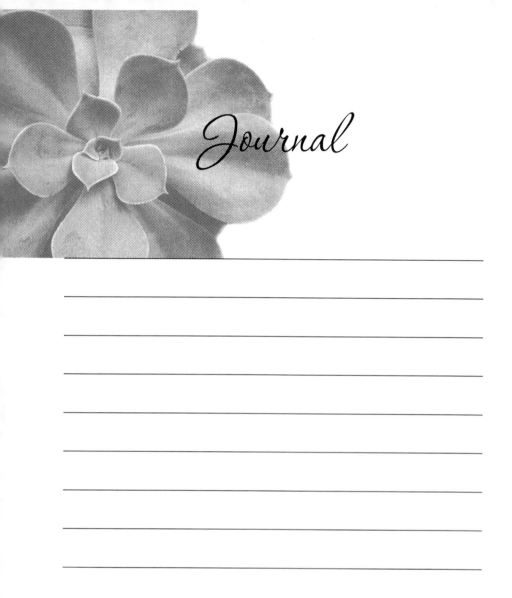

Journal

...of being seen and heard.

JOURNAL PROMPT

Do you value yourself enough to use your voice? How can you use your voice to speak up and create the life you envision for yourself? You deserve to be seen and heard, not brushed off, quieted, or pushed to the side.

Take a bold step with a trustworthy friend and voice one of your desires for your life. What we believe and proclaim, we see. God is faithful, even if life doesn't look the way we were expecting.

SCRIPTURE
Acts 18:9–10

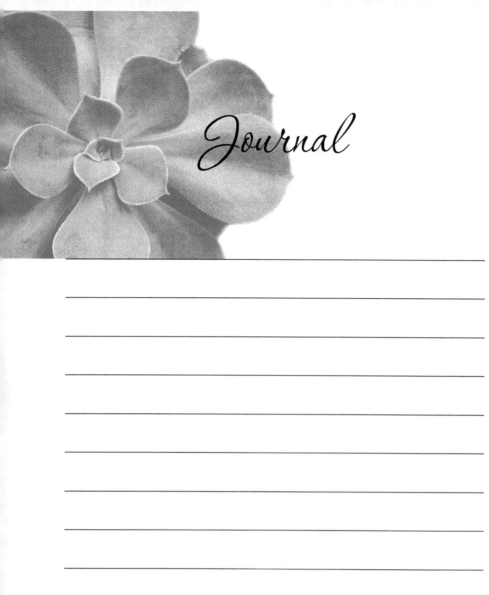

Journal

_____

_____

_____

_____

_____

_____

_____

_____

_____

_____

_____

_____

_____

_____

_____

_____

...of forgiving myself.

JOURNAL PROMPT

Have you made decisions you regret? Are there things you've done that have brought you to a place where you feel broken and lost? Are there things you can change in order to keep from going down this road again?

Reframe a specific situation by asking how you either benefitted or learned from that experience. Forgiving ourselves begins with taking personal responsibility as we learn to own our problems and make changes moving forward.

SCRIPTURE
Hebrews 4:16

Journal

...of being enough.

JOURNAL PROMPT

Do you compare yourself to others often? Comparison is the quickest way to find discontentment with your life. Ask yourself why your own life doesn't hold enough allure for you to be invested fully. Are there things that need to change?

Remind yourself that you will never know someone else's entire story. Give yourself permission to focus on your own story today. Write out ways you have grown in the last year, as well as things you would like to improve upon this year.

SCRIPTURE
Psalm 23:1–6

Journal

...of setting healthy boundaries.

JOURNAL PROMPT

What are some boundaries you think would be beneficial but you've been too intimidated to implement? Are there relationships that need healthier boundaries, whether with family or friends? What would that look like?

Setting healthy boundaries is not easy. When we do so, it changes everything. However, if there are unhealthy boundaries in your life, I'm willing to bet that you're uncomfortable with how things are. Why not let that discomfort spur you into a different discomfort – setting healthy boundaries – that has the potential to bring about great benefits in your relationship.

SCRIPTURE
Psalm 119:32–40

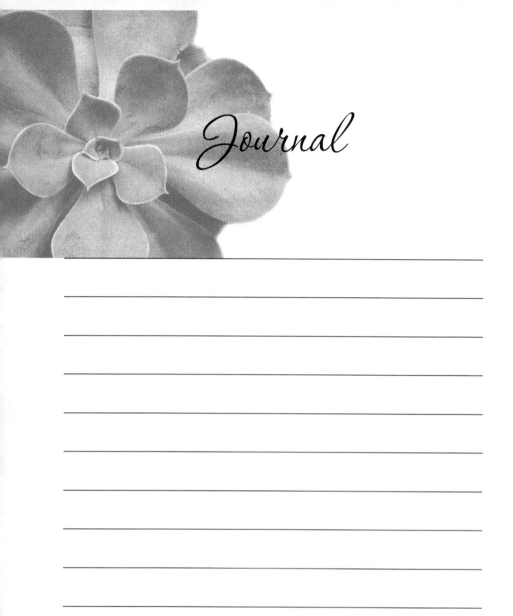

Journal

...of joy.

JOURNAL PROMPT

When was the last time you felt joyful—not just happy, but *joyful*—despite what turmoil is going on in and around you?

Define *joyful* and take time this week to discover one thing about your life that brings you joy. Consider activities, social justice causes, relationships, spirituality, and so on. Joy points to our internal state of being – our spirit – not just our current situations.

SCRIPTURE
John 16:24

Journal

...of finding calm in the chaos.

JOURNAL PROMPT

How does chaos affect you? Do you bottle up your emotions and allow them to explode? Do you allow chaos to drive your actions and words? Do you take time to process any discomfort you feel?

Take a moment to breathe. Use this time to understand which pieces of your chaotic experiences are out of your control and which ones you can take ownership of and change. Once you can identify what is in your control, you can set everything else down that you have no influence over.

SCRIPTURE
Philippians 4:67

Journal

...of trusting what God thinks of me.

JOURNAL PROMPT

How often do you allow others' perceptions of you to influence the way you think, act, or talk? When was the last time you asked God what He thinks of you and then took the time to be silent and wait for a response?

Find some space for quiet today. Silence everything around you, and ask God what He thinks of you. Start by reading this week's scripture. Allow His words to bring comfort to your soul. Now, listen.

SCRIPTURE
Zephaniah 3:17

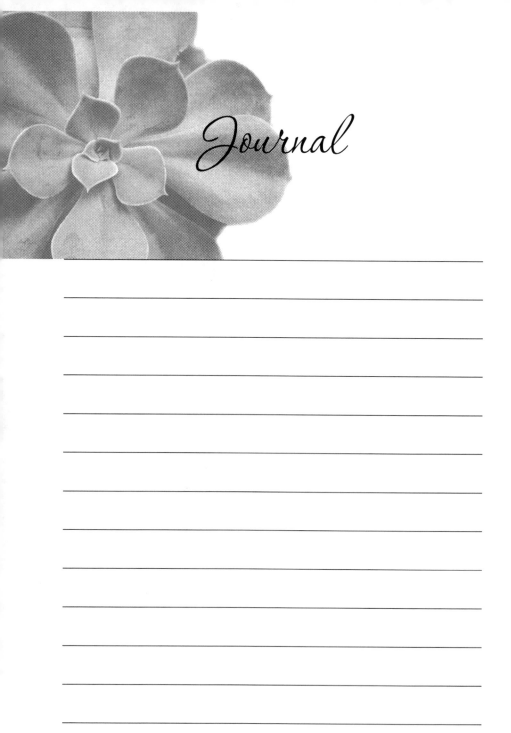

Journal

...of compassion.

JOURNAL PROMPT

How do you talk to yourself? Do you harbor any bitterness, anger, or unforgiveness in your heart against others or toward yourself?

Be mindful of ways you can recognize compassion in your life—words of a friend, finding comfort in difficult times, words whispered into your soul during devotional times. Allow God to speak into your life this week, washing you in His grace and compassion. We cannot give away compassion if we cannot hold that same space for ourselves. It is okay for us to feel all of our emotions. There are no *good* or *bad* emotions, just counterproductive actions as a result of those emotions. Give your emotions space to be heard and seen and be compassionate toward your experience of them.

SCRIPTURE
Colossians 3:12

Journal

... of finding grace in my brokenness.

JOURNAL PROMPT

Do you regard yourself as broken with nothing to give? How can you allow your brokenness to help you identify with someone else?

We are imperfect beings. We were not created to have everything figured out. On the contrary—we were created to build relationships with others in the midst of our mess, allowing our vulnerabilities to create connection. Where in your life can you allow grace to cover your flaws and bring true connection with others?

SCRIPTURE
Jeremiah 18:1–6

Journal

...of healthy communication.

JOURNAL PROMPT

How often do you invest in your relationships? Are you investing into your relationships in the same way you hope for in return?

Healthy communication starts with modeling healthy expectations and boundaries. How can you model health in your relationships? Be intentional in your relationships this week. Pick up the phone, start a dialogue, air a grievance, or have a laugh or cry. Healthy communication is most effective when we are willing to be vulnerable and honest.

SCRIPTURE
Colossians 4:6

Journal

...of hope.

JOURNAL PROMPT

Where do you find your hope? Is it anchored in fleeting things and feelings, the very things that are fluid and shift at a moment's notice? Or is it grounded and secured in the One who is steadfast and faithful?

Dig into your source of hope and remind yourself that you are not in this alone. We have the assurance that God is our hope, and He is steadfast through life's storms. He is the One who fills us with hope as we continually look to and trust in Him.

SCRIPTURE
Romans 15:13

Journal

_____

_____

_____

_____

_____

_____

_____

_____

_____

_____

_____

_____

_____

_____

_____

_____

...of having my needs met.

JOURNAL PROMPT

Do you put others' needs before your own, causing resentments down the line? Do you feel you can't ask for what you need? Do you value yourself, your words, and your time? Do your actions and behaviors reflect how you value yourself?

Take time to assess what you need—in relationships, faith, family, workplace, and on your healing journey. Practice vocalizing those needs. Know that your needs are valid! It's time to discover your worth and live like it.

SCRIPTURE
2 Timothy 1:6–7

Journal

...of giving myself healthy opportunities.

JOURNAL PROMPT

What are you afraid of? What keeps you from taking risks in your life? Do you open yourself up to opportunities or believe that you aren't worth things changing for?

If fear is holding you back, stop and ask yourself what good things fear is causing you to miss out on. Are you ready to allow those opportunities for growth to pass you by?

SCRIPTURE
Galatians 6:10

Journal

...of believing in myself.

JOURNAL PROMPT

What keeps you from believing in yourself? Fear, a lack of confidence, insecurities? What about your own inner critic or false beliefs about yourself?

Approach today's challenges with an open mind and a sense of curiosity. Ask those close to you for fresh ideas to help you recognize any unhelpful mindsets that may be keeping you from believing in your abilities, knowledge, and calling.

SCRIPTURE
Ephesians 2:8–9

Journal

...*of validation.*

JOURNAL PROMPT

How often do you feel like you're misunderstood or that your feelings are minimized? Do you feel this sets you up to be performative instead of genuine in your actions?

We need to stop living to please others. Pleasing others gives them power in your life. When our self-worth is found and grounded in God, we learn that we were fearfully and wonderfully made. Our lives are meant to please the One who created us. His care in creating us proves His undying love for us.

SCRIPTURE
Psalm 139:14

Journal

...of seeking help.

JOURNAL PROMPT

When was the last time you asked for help and felt its impact? What was it about that moment? Was the space you were in nonjudgmental? Was the person you were talking with empathetic or a good listener? Do you need someone close or someone who can be objective and see things from a different perspective?

Find someone who will meet you with objectivity and grace. Show yourself that you are worthy, *even when* you need to ask for help. There is nothing wrong with needing an extra hand along the way. It shows you know your limits well enough to know when you need some assistance.

SCRIPTURE
1 Corinthians 10:13

Journal

...of finding my strength.

JOURNAL PROMPT

What are your three greatest strengths? Are they easy to identify? Ask friends or family if you're having difficulty.

Write down specific examples of how these strengths are evident in your life. What would it look like if you were more intentional in how you define *strength*? Would that open the door to new possibilities? Use these strengths as a catalyst for your well-being and to create healthy perspectives of your capabilities.

SCRIPTURE
Romans 8:37

Journal

... of thoughtfulness.

JOURNAL PROMPT

Do you put as much thoughtfulness into yourself as you do your career, your relationships, your tasks? Do your actions show that you believe yourself to be an afterthought?

Be thoughtful about one thing regarding yourself today. Consider yourself as someone who is intentionally thought of by the Creator of this world, not as a mere afterthought. How can you shift your perspective of yourself to someone who is loved and thought about instead of one who is merely an afterthought?

SCRIPTURE
Psalm 8:3–9

Journal

...of being chosen.

JOURNAL PROMPT

When was the last time you experienced rejection? It's painful, and it feels defeating. Now think of a time when you were specifically chosen for something. How did that make you feel?

The great thing about being chosen by God is that it doesn't happen based on our merits. This week, I just want you to think about this statement—you were chosen by God before you could prove your worth. God never needs our achievements to justify His decision to choose us. You just have to trust and believe that you were made for a purpose.

SCRIPTURE
Ephesians 1:4

Journal

...of feeling safe.

JOURNAL PROMPT

What, where, or with whom is your safe space? Describe the emotions you experience and your thoughts when you feel safe.

If you don't have a safe space, take note of the people you can talk to and the places where you feel you can relax and be yourself. Take time to talk with God, and see what safety feels like with Him. Dig into His Word and see how often He is referred to as our refuge. How can God be your refuge this week?

SCRIPTURE
Proverbs 18:10

Journal

...of being patient with myself.

JOURNAL PROMPT

What does your self-talk sound like? Are you your biggest critic? Do you afford other people more patience than you afford yourself? Write down the thoughts you have when you lose patience with yourself.

Pay attention to your self-talk this week. Recognize when you become frustrated with yourself and step back to breathe. Ask yourself why you feel you don't deserve to treat yourself with patience and care.

SCRIPTURE
Galatians 6:9

Journal

...*of grieving in a healthy way*.

JOURNAL PROMPT

What are your expectations of grief? Do you feel you are able to express your emotions as you need to? What or who shaped your perception of grief?

When we grieve, we need to learn to fight for joy in the midst of our pain. First, find opportunities to seek refuge in God so you can receive rest. Second, make the Psalms a second home. Third, lean into close relationships. Do not buy into the lie that you need to grieve alone. We are made to live life together, even in all of life's messiness.

SCRIPTURE
Psalm 34:18

Journal

...of growth.

JOURNAL PROMPT

In what areas of your life do you want to see growth? How are you investing in that growth?

Write down the areas in your life in which you are wanting to experience growth. What steps can you take now to start making changes? Ask God to guide you in your next steps and reveal any barriers in your thought process that keep you from believing you are worthy of change.

SCRIPTURE
1 Timothy 4:15–16

Journal

...of healing.

JOURNAL PROMPT

Have you been praying or hoping for a miracle in your life? What does healing look like to you? What does healing *mean* to you?

Begin by writing down your expectations for what healing looks like for you. Consider the possibility that your definition may need to be reframed—you may have received healing in a different way than you were expecting.

SCRIPTURE
Psalm 103:2–4

Journal

...of creating a validating space for my emotions.

JOURNAL PROMPT

Do you know how to allow your emotions space to be felt and heard without allowing them to influence your actions and behaviors? What would it look like to be able to feel what you need to feel without letting those feelings run the entire show?

Find a quiet space and set a timer for five to ten minutes. Use this space to allow your feelings to be heard and acknowledged without judgment. This is not a space to find ways to resolve anything. Say to yourself, "I acknowledge that I feel *upset, sad, disappointed, etc.* and that's okay." Emotions are not bad. We need to address them as neutrals and not facts. Once the timer goes off, speak to your emotions, and say, "You have had space to be heard. Now it's time for me to continue with my day." The more our emotions are validated and heard, the easier it is for us to allow them to pass along without creating a disturbance.

SCRIPTURE
Psalm 6:4–9

Journal

...of having peace in my life.

JOURNAL PROMPT

Have you gotten into such chaotic habits in your life that peace feels unattainable or even unwanted at times? Peace can feel elusive, especially when you feel unworthy.

What is peace to you? Think through what it means to be at peace. Acknowledge the space that peace holds in your life. Anchor your peace in things above as well as in God's promises, no matter how crazy life gets. God assured us that He is with us through life's storms, so it shouldn't surprise us when we face those moments. Continue to look to Him and trust that He will guide you.

SCRIPTURE
Isaiah 26:3

Journal

...of meaning what I say.

JOURNAL PROMPT

How confident are you in what you say?
Do you find yourself saying something
or agreeing to something just to
change your answer later? Do you
believe that your behavior is rooted
in a desire to please others?

The more genuinely we lead
our lives, the more we don't
live in the discrepancies that
lie between our words and our
actions. Whatever you do, let your
yes be *yes* and your *no* be *no*.

SCRIPTURE
Matthew 5:37

Journal

...of dispelling my doubts and anxieties.

JOURNAL PROMPT

Do you allow your anxieties and worries to take over and commandeer your life? How would your life look if you looked at situations through a different lens other than your anxiety?

Ask yourself this question every time you feel anxious or worried about a situation: What would be different if I weren't anxious or worried? How would this situation look to me then?

SCRIPTURE
Philippians 4:6–8

Journal

...of surrounding myself with good friends.

JOURNAL PROMPT

Do you have people in your corner? People you can learn from and grow with? People you can be your *genuine self* with?

Find and focus on relationships with those who can share their wins, losses, and authenticity with you. We were created to live life in relationship with others. Iron sharpens iron.

SCRIPTURE
Proverbs 27:17

Journal

...of knowing my value.

JOURNAL PROMPT

What does it mean to have value? Do your actions show that you find value in yourself? Do you feel inherently kind, compassionate, and respectful of others? Do you feel worthy of those same things in return, or do you see yourself through the eyes of people who don't value you?

You were created with inherent value and worth. You are valuable enough for Someone to die for and crave a relationship with! The gospel reveals your undeniable value.

SCRIPTURE
1 Peter 2:9

Journal

...of change.

JOURNAL PROMPT

Are there areas in your life where you want to see change? What would it take to create change in your life? How hard is change for you?

Not all change is bad. It's hard, undoubtedly, but not all bad. Change allows you to grow, to reveal new facets of who you are, and to learn new things. Identify the emotions you associate with change and lean into them without judgment. Discover how these emotions have influenced your personal view of change.

SCRIPTURE
2 Corinthians 5:17

Journal

...of being still.

JOURNAL PROMPT

Do you find it difficult to be still? To quiet your mind and focus on God's voice? Do you feel you deserve to take a break and breathe, to take note of your emotions and decompress?

When we learn to be still, we can begin to tune into God's voice. Begin to listen and see what God is directing you toward in your daily life. See what changes in direction and focus He's bringing to your attention in this space.

SCRIPTURE
Psalm 46:10

Journal

...of processing negative emotions.

JOURNAL PROMPT

What negative emotions do you avoid? What negative emotions do you need to let go of? What negative emotions do you need to write down and work through later?

Identify your emotions and give them time to be heard in a non-judgmental space. The more we try to avoid and push away our negative emotions, the more aggressively they want to be heard. Giving these emotions space doesn't mean we have to act on them, but it does allow us to acknowledge them and begin the work of processing them in a healthy way.

SCRIPTURE
Matthew 21:22

Journal

...of belonging.

JOURNAL PROMPT

To belong means to be rightly placed in a specified position. What if you are focusing more on making yourself fit in instead of relying on God's masterful ability to place you where you need to be? Look at Esther in scripture. What if you were made for such a time as this because God made you uniquely qualified for your role as she was?

Stop looking for ways to fit in this week. Instead, look at the abilities God gave you to be able to speak life into the environment you're in.

SCRIPTURE
Esther 4:14

Journal

...of knowing my limits.

JOURNAL PROMPT

Are you good at taking on everything, thinking that your way is best or most efficient? Do you often feel overwhelmed or overworked? Can you recognize when you are doing too much, and can you ask for help? What keeps you from reaching out before you've reached your limit?

When we acknowledge our limitations, we allow God to step in and take control. We learn to recognize that not everything can be accomplished in our own strength. Use your approaching exhaustion as a gauge to tell you when you're operating beyond your capacity. Only then can you begin the work of setting new boundaries for yourself.

SCRIPTURE
James 4:10

Journal

...of being in control of my responses.

JOURNAL PROMPT

What triggers the emotions that make you feel out of control? How do you feel after you've made a decision based on an emotional response?

God created you with the ability to think things through, no matter how you may feel in the moment. He wants you to use your wisdom. Your wisdom is there to tell you to wait a little while until your emotions settle down, then check to see if you really believe your initial emotional reaction is the right thing to do. Don't let your emotions hurry you into making poor decisions.

SCRIPTURE
Proverbs 16:32

Journal

...of using kind and respectful self-talk.

JOURNAL PROMPT

Do you find that you are your biggest critic and judge? What words do you find echoing in your mind when you make a mistake? Do these words match who you believe you truly are?

Write down your negative thoughts this week. Then write down how you talk to yourself in response to these thoughts. Once you identify your self-talk, you can begin to replace your negative self-talk with positive truths about yourself that you have uncovered in your relationship with God.

SCRIPTURE
Ephesians 4:29

Journal

...of ridding my life of unhealthy habits.

JOURNAL PROMPT

Do you find yourself attached to something unhealthy? What does this say about your needs that may be going unmet? What is this negative attachment doing for you? What about the situation is within your control to change?

Our thought processes play so much into what we do. If you find yourself justifying others' contributions in your life, it may be time to reevaluate those relationships. See what, or who, may no longer be beneficial to you.

SCRIPTURE
Ephesians 4:22–24

Journal

...of learning new things about myself.

JOURNAL PROMPT

What is it like to be curious about yourself instead of critical?

Write about what you see in the mirror. Write down the words that you need to hear. Be curious about things you don't yet know about yourself. Start asking yourself who has the most influence in your life. Who has the ability to speak life or death into your life?

SCRIPTURE
1 John 2:27

Journal

...of making myself a priority.

JOURNAL PROMPT

What thoughts flood your mind when you talk about making yourself a priority? Where do you fit into your priority list? What do you do to ensure that your needs are met so you can be a genuine resource to others?

You can't take care of anyone else unless you take care of yourself first. Your health is a priority in order to be spiritually, emotionally, intellectually, and physically available to others.

SCRIPTURE
Luke 5:16

Journal

...of accepting compliments.

JOURNAL PROMPT

Reflect on the skills and personal qualities you are working to improve. What do you hope to be recognized for in the future - accomplishments, character traits, and so on? What are you doing to develop these things? Why are they meaningful to you?

Begin a gratitude journal by listing three things you are grateful for every day. Practice showing gratitude for the good things about yourself and your life as the first step toward accepting compliments. This will allow you to internalize the good things said about you instead of negating them.

SCRIPTURE
Proverbs 27:2

Journal

...of being courageous.

JOURNAL PROMPT

Examining ourselves and our emotions takes a great deal of courage. *Why do I feel unworthy of love? Why does their comment hurt so deeply? Why did their actions affect my emotions and behaviors?*

Asking ourselves the right questions allows us to unlock our inner courage. It takes a lot to dive into ourselves and seek the truth in our own lives. Allow God to speak to your heart and show you that courage isn't the absence of fear, rather it's knowing how to push past the lies that tell you you're not worthy of making progress.

SCRIPTURE
Joshua 1:9

Journal

...of not being defined by my struggles.

JOURNAL PROMPT

What do you focus on more—your struggles or successes? How can you reframe your struggles to expose the strengths you gained in the process?

Write down your current struggles. Now, next to your struggles, write down what you've learned through those struggles. The more we reframe our difficult moments to expose the truth and discover the strengths we possess, the more ready and willing we are to begin believing the truth that we are uniquely designed to navigate our struggles.

SCRIPTURE
Proverbs 18:10

Journal

...of unapologetically being me.

JOURNAL PROMPT

How often do you allow others to dictate who you are? Do you follow what others want to do by not speaking up for yourself? Do you voice your own opinions, or do you find yourself apologizing for your thoughts? Do you know what makes you *you*?

Make it your goal to not apologize for anything you say this week. Be courageous enough to take up space. Do what you say, and say what you mean. This is your time to give yourself the freedom to be unapologetically you!

SCRIPTURE
Romans 8:5–6

Journal

...of identifying my emotions.

JOURNAL PROMPT

Are you good at identifying your emotions beyond the base emotions of sadness, happiness, anger, and fear? What lies beneath those base emotions?

God examines our thoughts and emotions. This shows His deep love and care for who you are, not just what you do. It is your job to dig beneath your base emotions to discover what is truly happening with your deeper feelings. It is only through doing so that you are able to identify feelings of vulnerability, unworthiness, or of being unsafe. Emotional honesty connects us with God, ourselves, and others.

SCRIPTURE
Ecclesiastes 3:1–8

Journal

...of breaking cycles.

JOURNAL PROMPT

Do you feel stuck in unhealthy cycles of dysfunctional emotions and behaviors? Have you created unhealthy responses to protect yourself? Are these responses based in generational family patterns?

Often we cling to what is comfortable because the unknown is uncomfortable. Pray for God to show you what cycles you need to break or give Him control of.

SCRIPTURE
Ezekiel 18:19–20

Journal

...of rest and chocolate.

JOURNAL PROMPT

What would it look like if you cared for yourself as well as you care for others?

Do one thing to care for yourself today. You can't pour from an empty cup. Resting, identifying emotions, and connecting with God and others is vital to your mental, emotional, physical, and spiritual wellbeing.

SCRIPTURE
Matthew 11:28

Journal

... *of* _____ .

_____

JOURNAL PROMPT

It's your turn to fill in the blank. After fifty-one weeks of journaling through *I am worthy of* statements, what has God spoken to you? What are you worthy of?

Take time to allow God to speak to you this week. What have you learned in this journey of self-discovery that can lead you to better define your self-worth?

SCRIPTURE
Matthew 16:25

Journal

Journal

_____

_____

_____

_____

_____

_____

_____

_____

_____

_____

_____

_____

_____

_____

_____

_____

Journal

Journal

Scripture References:

Ephesians 2:4–9

Proverbs 24:27

Romans 12:2

Romans 5:6–11

Acts 18:9–10

Hebrews 4:16

Psalm 23:1–6

Psalm 119:32–40

John 16:24

Philippians 4:6–7

Zephaniah 3:17

Colossians 3:12

Jeremiah 18:1–6

Colossians 4:6

Romans 15:13

2 Timothy 1:6–7

Galatians 6:10

Ephesians 2:8–9

Psalm 139:14

1 Corinthians 10:13

Romans 8:37

Psalm 8:3–9

Ephesians 1:4

Proverbs 18:10

Galatians 6:9

Psalm 34:18

Scripture References:

1 Timothy 4:15–16

Psalm 103:2–4

Psalm 6:4-9

Isaiah 26:3

Matthew 5:37

Philippians 4:6–8

Proverbs 27:17

1 Peter 2:9

2 Corinthians 5:17

Psalm 46:10

Matthew 21:22

Esther 4:14

James 4:10

Proverbs 16:32

Ephesians 4:29

Ephesians 4:22–24

1 John 2:27

Luke 5:16

Proverbs 27:2

Joshua 1:9

Proverbs 18:10

Romans 8:5–6

Ecclesiastes 3:1–8

Ezekiel 18:19–20

Matthew 11:28

Matthew 16:25

Printed in the United States
by Baker & Taylor Publisher Services